Psychology Articles

How to build self-confidence

Branka Vasilev, psychologist

ISBN-10: 1478182644

ISBN-13: 978-1478182641

DEDICATION

To my husband and son for their love and support

PREFACE

This book offers 19 tips – activities based on the knowledge of psychology, whose implementation can help you boost your self-confidence. It is designed for those who want to do something towards building their self-confidence without paying for the services of a psychologist or a psychotherapist. It is a good guide for those who want to do something more and better than what they have already achieved in their life, who want to exploit their full potential and achieve more success at work, studies, in love, marriage and parenting. On the one hand, this manual describes daily problems in life which are a direct consequence of the lack of self-confidence. On the other hand, it provides detailed guidance by which a person should manage their life in order to boost their self-confidence, and draws attention to the benefits of being self-confident. This guide is a result of six years of experience which the author gained during her work as a psychologist, giving advice and searching for a solution to a wide range of problems people are beset with.

CONTENTS

1 WHAT IS SELF-CONFIDENCE?

The word self-confidence means our ability to trust ourselves, or the ability to rely on ourselves and our potential. In other words, self-confident people are satisfied with themselves and have faith in their abilities.

Self-confidence is not something inborn. All of us come into this world with a preference for developing certain personality traits, which are usually classified into two broad types of behavior: extroverted and introverted. Nowadays it seems that, from a social and an intellectual point of view, extroverted children have a greater chance of success. However, extroversion is not a guarantee of strong self-confidence. Self-confidence is built and developed throughout the whole life. The way we raise our children has a great impact on the development of their self-confidence, which means that parents play the crucial role in creating the basis for self-confidence in their children. For example, newborn babies do not suffer from a lack of self-confidence at all. They cry from the top of their lungs asking for what they need. However, during the first months of its life, the baby builds confidence depending on how the mother meets the infant's needs. A mother who immediately responds to her baby's cry by taking it into her arms, feeding it when it is hungry, changing its diapers when it is wet and always meeting its needs, contributes to the development of the baby's sense of self-confidence. On the contrary, a mother who usually does not respond to baby's crying or reacts with a delay contributes to a feeling of distrust in her baby. Over time, as the child grows, it absorbs all praises, complaints, reprimands and comments of its parents. The child builds up an attitude towards itself which is based on its parents attitude, their words and the way they treat the child. Parents who usually criticize their son, who ignore or downplay the significance of his achievements and overreact when he makes a mistake, put him to shame, belittle him, call him names, tell him that he is not good, exert a very negative influence on the development of his self-confidence. Such treatment leads to children growing up into individuals with low self-confidence, who are insecure and anxious, in other words, children who send out a poor image of themselves. But it's not only their parents: their family, friends, neighbors, teachers and coaches also have a major impact on the development of children's confidence in both negative and positive terms.

2 THE LACK OF SELF-CONFIDENCE IS THE ROOT OF MANY PROBLEMS IN LIFE

Communication problems

People with low self-confidence generally assume that others are better, prettier and smarter than them and behave as if they were worthless. Instead of considering themselves as equal participants in communication, they remain in the background, as if other people's needs were more important than theirs, as if others had more rights. They do not dare to clearly and directly express their opinions and feelings for fear of rejection or condemnation. They feel uncertain and it is very important for them to be accepted by others. Because of that, they feel very uncomfortable when they have to express their opinion in public. They excessively compare themselves to others and often feel ashamed. Here is an example:

Mark says: "Can you please lend me some money to fix my car? I'll give it back to you the as soon as I get my salary". Alex answers: "You know, we're repairing our house… We're having huge expenses… (He hesitates to say openly: "I am not in a position to lend you the money because it is intended for the repair of our family home".) Mark is confident and keeps pushing on without worrying about how Alex would react: "I wouldn't have asked you if I weren't in trouble. I really need my car fixed. Besides, I have already told you, I will give it back to you as soon as my salary comes in." Alex is still insecure and replies: "Well, I don't know… (though he knows very well that he cannot give him the money), I can't promise you anything… I need to talk to my wife…" (this way he gives an impression as if there is still a possibility of lending him the money and Mark will continue with his request the next day, the day after tomorrow and so on…).

Relationship problems

By being insecure and having difficulties in communication, people with low self-confidence often have problems in intimate relationships. Due to the lack of self-confidence people stay in unhealthy relationships or marriages, often missing great opportunities for love and failing to find a suitable partner because they wait for someone to approach them rather than initiating a date themselves.   Moreover, those who managed to find a suitable partner often have a fear of emotional attachment which is certainly not good for any relationship. They are afraid of intimacy and are not able to open up to their partner because they believe that he/she would become aware of their weaknesses and leave them.

Problems at school or work

Students with low self-confidence are usually withdrawn and reticent, they remain in the shadow, and often stay unnoticed even though they do have sufficient knowledge, skills and abilities. They are unobtrusive and do not know how to show their qualities and skills, in other words, they suffer from a lack of self-representation. These are usually students who speak up only if they are absolutely sure that they know the correct answer. If they are not absolutely certain, they are more likely to stay silent than give the wrong answer and be ridiculed, all of which affects their grades. Because of that, they are usually more successful in written tests than oral exams. Persons with low self-confidence find it harder to fit into a group and they don't know how to fight for their place in a team, both at school and at work.

They lack the strength to stand up for their rights and assert themselves in front of others. These are people who hesitate to ask for a raise, who find it difficult to say "no" when it is necessary – for example, to reject a new task because they are already overloaded with work. It is difficult for them to accept an assignment or a challenging responsible position because they are afraid they might fail to meet the expectations of the new position. They often keep an inadequate position or a job although they are dissatisfied, simply out of fear that they will not be able to find a better one.

People with low self-esteem are often victims of violence and abuse

People with low self-esteem are more often victims of abuse and violence than those with high self-esteem, because they feel helpless and think they can do nothing to protect themselves. Remember the time when you were a student. There was probably a boy who was a victim and who was being beaten and ridiculed by other kids. This boy was most likely withdrawn, insecure and lonely. He wasn't aggressive, nor did he provoke others, he only kept to himself, and yet he was beaten up and mocked. Aggressive boys recognized him as a potential victim just because he was insecure and lonely, because he didn't have anyone to defend him, and they knew that he would not fight back. The same goes for victims of mobbing at workplace.

Health problems

The lack of self-confidence causes the feelings of loneliness and anxiety. People with low self-confidence are too anxious and always afraid of what might happen if they make a mistake, if they fail or become a laughing-stock. Their anxieties, fears and feelings are pent up inside because of the difficulty to open up to others. Loneliness, dissatisfaction, isolation, uncertainty and anxiety (all kept inside) make them less resistant to stress, which can be a trigger for many diseases. All this leads also to a greater risk of substance abuse (drugs, alcohol), depression and similar problems. Furthermore, if dissatisfaction and the negative self-image get increased, it could lead to self-destructive ideas.

3 HOW TO BUILD SELF-CONFIDENCE

Building and maintaining self-confidence is a difficult task because it is not enough to simply make this decision; it is necessary to be persistent and work on it every day. Just like doing physical exercises in order to build up muscles.

We are all born with a certain potential. If we do not develop these resources, a sense of unhappiness, dissatisfaction and a negative self-image will occur and consequently the lack of self-confidence and self-esteem. Our self-confidence needs to be strengthened by developing our potential, by continuously struggling to improve our skills, knowledge and qualities. That way we "grow" as a person. Our environment could help us to develop our potential, but it might also hinder us. Nevertheless, we are responsible for our own development regardless of the difficulties and obstacles that surround us. The fact that someone didn't have adequate external conditions (e.g. adequate parents) to facilitate the development of their potential cannot be used as an excuse and doesn't absolve them of responsibility for their own development, despite the obstacles, risks, the pain and suffering that are an integral part of life. Although this is not easy, it is nevertheless a fact that we really can do a lot to boost our self-confidence. The potential that we have is a kind of our capital for success. By using it effectively and with a clear aim in our mind, we stand a good chance of achieving what we want and becoming successful. Without a feeling of success you cannot build up your self-confidence and you should therefore strive for success and catch that feeling. Remember that the feeling of success really motivates and boosts self-confidence. Because of that, people who are already successful are more motivated to achieve new victories.

4   19 TIPS FOR BUILDING SELF-CONFIDENCE

1. There is no good start without a strong motivation

I am sure that reading this guide will help most people to strengthen their self-confidence. But there will be those who will read this book, and not make any practical steps to build their self-confidence. Why is this so? Why do some people gain more benefit after reading this manual than others who have less or even no benefit from it? What does it depend on? It depends on the motivation of each of you. Someone is more motivated, and someone less. The greater the dissatisfaction with your self-confidence is and the more problems you have, the stronger the motivation to strengthen your self-confidence will be. Those who believe that it would be good to boost their self-confidence, but who are still doing well in their everyday life, are less motivated and will read this guide just out of curiosity. But, remember, motivation is essential to fuel every preferred step in life. Some of you have already realized that the lack of self-confidence creates many problems in everyday life and are firmly resolved to persevere and to succeed in finally strengthening it. Some of you are already determined to do it seriously and are dedicated to this task. These persons will not only read this manual and give up. They will start applying what they have read in this guide and keep it in mind every moment of every day. If you are persistent and consistent, you will succeed, that much is certain.

2. Get to know yourself better and accept yourself as you are

If you know yourself well, if you know your strengths and limitations, if you have a good communication with yourself, you will be able to rely on yourself more. People are often afraid to be themselves for fear of rejection. They care too much about other people's opinion and behave in a certain way in order to make sure that they feel like they belong to a particular group and they often do what others want them to in order to be loved and accepted. They always try to meet other people's needs and often neglect their own needs. But this is so devastating for their self-confidence! Self-confidence is not built through a comparison with other people because no matter how good we are, there will always be someone better, prettier and more successful. Instead of comparing yourself with others, you should compare yourself with your own personality over the years. Ask yourself: "How much progress did I make today compared to yesterday, last month, last year or last ten years?" So stick to the goals that you consider valuable, instead of copying others. Remember, people are subjective and no matter how hard you try to make a good impression, they will generally see what they want to see.

Self-acceptance is the first step in the process of self-improvement because it will open the door to new possibilities for you. People who have a problem with self-acceptance and tend to keep the situation such as it is will be "cemented" in the past. A good example is a person who cannot accept an end to a relationship. He/she is not able to accept that the relationship didn't work and that it was the cause of the break up. He/she continues to mourn for years after the break up convincing him/herself that the right person would never come. That way, this person misses out on many important opportunities in life.

Another example are women who do not accept their age. Struggling with getting older, they subject themselves to facelifting, but soon become dissatisfied again and wish to correct their nose, lips, breasts and so on. They remain trapped in the days of youth struggling to accept the change instead of enjoying the present and all the blessings of life.

What to do then? First, listen to your feelings. Ask yourself, which activities make you feel happy and satisfied? What qualities about yourself are you most proud of? Which people usually contribute to your good mood? The answers to these questions can help you look into yourself more clearly. Moreover, they can help you see if your desires are absolutely yours and not the wishes and expectations of other people. This is very important, because the feeling of happiness arises when we achieve something that is important to us.

3. Dream about the life that you would like to have

Imagine that your resources are not limited by anything, what kind of life would you like for yourself and your family? What would you like to do? What would you look like? How much money would you earn? How would your relationship look like? How many children would you like to have? Where would you like to travel?

The clearer your vision of happiness is, the faster you will move towards health and success. Dreaming of yourself as a happy and successful person contributes to a better self-image and directly increases your self-confidence. There is something about these dreams and visions that encourages people to get started and gradually, little by little, accomplish things that lead them to making those dreams come true.

4. Learn how to make decisions

People with low self-confidence have difficulties in making decisions. They are afraid of making mistakes, they always hesitate and finally often decide it is better not to make any decisions at all. It is the safer option to them, because taking any action carries along some risk. They something think like this: "Better the devil you know than the angel you don't know". Unlike them, self-confident people are determined and action-oriented. They do more things in one day and their life changes faster. During their lifetime, they make much more decisions than people with low self-confidence. Because they make more decisions, they try out more different things in life. The more they try, the better chance they actually have of finding a way to achieve their goals. Thus self-confident people are more successful.

So, instead of being passive and waiting for things to just happen or letting others make decisions for you, you have to start making decisions of your own. Having made a decision of your own, you will also make one step towards increased self-confidence. All of us feel important and powerful when we are in a position to decide on something. You have to remember that everyone holds their decisions much dearer and prefer them, even if they turn out wrong, than the decisions that others make for them.

5. Be active

Confident and successful people are active. They don't wait for things to happen, but take steps to reverse the situation to their advantage. They do not wait for favorable conditions in life, but they take action to create conditions that facilitate the achievement of their goals. Most people, especially those with low self-confidence, spring into action only when provoked by an external impulse. These actions are mere reactions to external stimuli. Such people often need to experience some horrible things, like disease, flooding, job loss, etc. to realize that they are indeed able to do something to turn the situation in their favor. Then they start to act, change and adapt themselves, and actively work to achieve their goals.

You have to remember: action leads to improved self-confidence, and on the contrary, inaction, hesitation and withdrawal lead to a loss of self-confidence. The more active we are and the more we achieve on the basis of our own decisions and efforts, the more motivated we will be for new goals, and gradually we will become more self-confident and more successful.

6. You must be willing to change yourself

This is not an easy task. People are generally difficult to change, because the change itself is neither easy nor pleasant. Many people do not have the strength of character or willingness to make a firm decision that they want to change. Usually they only make a decision to try to change. It is easy for them to decide that they want to change certain habits, but when it comes to implementing these changes, it finally turns out that they are not ready to give up old habits and the former way of life. They want to build their self-confidence, but they often give up because it is sometimes difficult and painful to change old habits and the way of life, and then they start looking for excuses.

In order to boost your self-confidence, you must give up some of the current habits in favor of some more adequate and meaningful ones. This change will facilitate the achievement of your goals (strengthening self-confidence) and it is very important to persevere with it. Every time you persevere in something (e.g. last month you endured in your determination not to light a cigarette, or you took a half an hour every day to learn Spanish), you appreciate yourself more and more. This ability of self-control is of great importance if you want to reach your goal. Self-discipline is one of the qualities of successful people. Although they are not willing or pleased to do some things at this very moment, they will nevertheless do it now, because they are aware that it pays off in the long run, and it's the price they must pay for the success that they want. One of their secrets is that every form of self-discipline reinforces other forms of discipline. The more you apply discipline in small things, the better you will be able to apply discipline that is required for major challenges like building self-confidence.

7. You must be persistent

Remember that there is not a single person who never doubts themselves and who always achieves everything they want. Everybody feels insecure sometimes and every one of us has experienced a failure, but that doesn't mean that you should give up. You should pursue all things that are important in your life, even when you are faced with obstacles and when you fail. Because, when you really want something and you believe you can achieve it, then you will find the way and means to attain your goals. Perseverance is a quality that accompanies all great successes in life.

What do you think, why successful people manage to be persistent and to persevere to the end? Here's the secret to their persistence. Successful people lead a dynamic life. They make many decisions and undertake a range of activities in order to fulfill their plans. Therefore they often face obstacles, difficulties and crises, much more than passive people who rarely take any action at all, and whose life is not dynamic. Due to this fact, successful people have more experience in overcoming crises and obstacles. They learned that the ups and downs are an inevitable part of life. So when they start carrying out their plans, they take into account the possible ups and downs and disappointments in advance, and if problems do come, these people are psychologically prepared to deal with them. Because of that, it is easier for them to be persistent and persevere to the very end. Even before the obstacle appears, their unconsciousness receives the information saying: "I will be persistent and persevere to the end despite the obstacles I encounter". Here's what Calvin Coolidge, the 30th President of the United States, said about persistence: "Nothing in the world can take the place of persistence. Talent will not: nothing is more common than unsuccessful men with talent. Genius will not: unrewarded genius is almost a proverb. Education will not: the world is full of educated derelicts. Persistence and determination alone are omnipotent. The slogan "Press On" has solved and always will solve the problems of the human race".

8. Replace negative thoughts with praise

People with low self-esteem are often unfairly hard on themselves. For example: "It seems that the guests liked my dinner because they emptied all the plates… (then comes self-criticism) Though many things were not as they should've been… I'm surprised they did not notice that the soup was not spicy enough… I'm so clumsy and forgetful". These negative thoughts should be replaced with the following ones: "It seems that the guests really liked my dinner. Maybe it was not perfect, but I really made an effort and prepared a delicious meal. For a beginner, this is quite a success. I'm so proud of myself!" Here is another example: "She didn't say anything, but apparently she did not like the bouquet… When she opened the door she was not happy, which means that she didn't like the bouquet... I'm just not good with women". These negative thoughts should be replaced with: "I noticed that she was not happy, but I don't know why. Perhaps it had nothing to do with me or the bouquet. Maybe there is something bothering her. It's best to ask her why she wasn't happy".

As seen in these examples, everything you say to yourself, the inner monologue, influences the strengthening or weakening of your self-confidence. So in a certain situation, when your confidence is badly needed (for example, when you want to come up to a girl/boy), you alone can weaken your own confidence if you tell yourself: "I'm not that good for her/him, he/she will definitely reject me". In this situation, what will help you is the inner monologue as follows: "Girls love guys (and vice versa) who have the guts to make the first move. It impresses them. I'm dressed nicely and I have devised tactics, so I stand a good chance of success".

Always keep in mind that in most situations (exams, job interviews, public speaking, courting, sports competitions…), the worst that can happen to you is to be rejected, ridiculed, disgraced or to fail. But remember, this is not the end of the world! Failure is common for everyone. Even the most successful people have experienced many failures in their lives. It's part of life. After all, if you are to regret something, it is certainly better to regret something that you have done then something you haven't.

9. Treat yourself as a valuable person

You have to reward yourself for success. It could be shopping, spending an evening with your family or friends, a day free of work… Do something for yourself that makes you feel special and really good. Diplomas, certificates, photographs you're proud of etc. should be kept at a visible spot to remind you of your accomplishments. The following exercise can be very useful:

Take a pen and paper and finish the following sentences:

1. What I have achieved in my life is...

2. I am proud of…

3. One of my best qualities is...

4. What I am good at and what I do well is...

Keep the paper with these sentences at a visible spot to be constantly reminded of you how good and valuable a person you are.

10. Surround yourself with the right people

It is immensely important which people you identify yourself and spend time with. Make sure that you surround yourself with positive and optimistic people who have a vision and goals and who are making progress in their lives. These could be people from your nearest surroundings: parents, friends, relatives, teachers... or public figures such as athletes, actors, writers... Of course, I do not think that you have to meet public figures in person. For example, you could read articles in papers about them and identify with some of their attitudes or be informed of their work, their way of life, the way they achieved success, and then apply that in your own life. Surround yourself with positive people, follow their example and it will be easier for you to persevere on your path to building self-confidence and being more successful. We all have a tendency to absorb the attitudes and the behavior of people we are surrounded with and spend most of the day with. There is a saying that goes: "If you want to fly with the eagles, don't go digging the ground with the turkeys", or the another one: "a man is known by the company he keeps."

One of the secrets of successful people is that they try to be surrounded by those who are better, more competent and successful in something. Those people simply motivate them to be also more successful. If you surround yourself with such people, and you are willing to cooperate, learn and make progress, you will have unlimited opportunities ahead. Here's what I was told by a girl who was not brilliant in high school, but at the faculty she achieved excellent results: "Coincidentally, from the first day of my studies, I hung out extensively with the four girls who were outstanding students. Through my friendship with them, I became even more interested in these studies. It was for the most part thanks to them that I became such a good student. If I hadn't fitted into their group I certainly would not have made such success."

Successful people tend to build, maintain and foster a high-quality network of social relations and often thanks to their acquaintances they achieve more than people who sit at home and watch TV all day long.

11. Don't hesitate to seek help and support of others

People with low self-confidence rarely seek help and support of others, and they are not aware that sometimes the help of others is just what they need to overcome the negative experiences from the past. Here's what could be helpful:

– Ask a friend of yours which of your traits they appreciate the most, what they like about you;

– Talk to someone who knows how to listen without judgment and criticism;

– Ask your coach or teacher to tell you what they think you are doing well;

– Attend courses on acquiring and enhancing self-confidence;

– Read books on topics related to self-confidence.

12. Set goals for yourself

One of the secrets of successful people is that they set goals for themselves and make plans how to achieve these goals. Unlike them, people without defined goals spend their time in vain because they do not have a sense of direction in life. There's nothing they must do today, they do not have deadlines that must be met and thus they become lazy and let themselves be carried by the rivers of life.

You must consider which activities you have to do every day, consistently and systematically in order to develop your skills and improve the quality of life. Ask yourself the following questions:

– How can I increase my work capacity and skills? What should I read, learn and which courses should I attend;

– What can I do to improve my health; What should I eat? Which sport should I take on? How long should I sleep?

– What can I do for my relationship? How much time should we spend together? How can I improve communication with my partner? What can I do to "refresh" our sex life and bring more romance into our daily routine?

– How to surround myself with self-confident and successful people and strengthen the existing friendships and business contacts? Where can I meet such people? Which activities could get me closer to them?

Take a paper and draw a vertical line across the middle. To the left, write down your goals. To the right, note down the same goals, but sort them out and number them by priority. Under number one, write down the goal that you need to realize first, the goal that is currently the most important for you. Having set your priorities right, try to organize your life and energy in accordance with these priorities. Set a deadline for each of these goals. Then, for each goal, make a comprehensive list of activities that should be done, and which lead to the achievement of the goals. Write down every idea you can think of that could lead to the accomplishment of your goals.

And yet, take care not to ask yourself to do impossible things. That way you will certainly not strengthen your self-confidence. It is very important to set goals that are realistic and attainable. The realization of each of these goals results in increased self-esteem and self-confidence that lead us to new challenges and successes. The more active we are and the more goals we achieve, the more successful we are going to be, and our self-confidence will strengthen more and more. Some larger goals (whose realization requires several years) should be split up into smaller goals and realized successively. With the realization of these goals, your sense of success will grow as well as the motivation to achieve the next, higher goals. Successful people continuously have their goals in mind and this results in making constant progress.

Thomas Carlyle, a Scottish satirical writer, essayist, historian and teacher, spoke about goals, obstacles and self-esteem:

"A man without a goal is like a ship without a rudder".

"Obstacles don't have to stop you. If you run into a wall, don't turn around and give up. Figure out how to climb it, go through it, or work around it".

"Nothing builds self-esteem and self-confidence like accomplishment".

13. Consider yourself responsible for your own life

Self-confident people show a high degree of self-responsibility. They consider themselves solely responsible for their health, career, family life, car, a pet... So, stop looking for excuses and blaming others for your own mistakes and incompetence. If there is something you don't like in your life, it is up to you whether you are going to change it. You are responsible for your own life. Take matters into your own hands. You are the boss.

14. Be an expert in the work you do

Whether you are a scientist, a craftsman or a police officer, make sure you're really good at what you do. Almost all self-confident, successful people consider themselves very competent in their field of work. None of them was born an expert, but they became experts because they were committed to excellence. If they managed to succeed, then you can also do it. You have unlimited power to learn and improve yourself. Competence in your field of work is very important for your self-confidence, self-esteem and pride, and it contributes to you feeling safer in relations with other people. You will also be more appreciated by others if they see you as a master of your business.

15. Use the power of your subconscious

In our subconscious we are the best, the brightest and the most beautiful, no matter what we knowingly say. We are the bosses of our own subconscious and it will always try to prove that what we say is the truth. Therefore, when you tell yourself: "I can do it", you are giving a positive impetus to your subconscious and it will do everything to prove that you are right. On the contrary, when you say: "I can't do it", you are giving a negative incentive to your subconscious. In that case, no matter how much you consciously try to do something, you're fighting against your own subconscious. Then your subconscious works against you because it received the information, "my boss (the boss is nobody else but you) said that it can't be done" and it tries to prove it right. Because of that, it is of paramount importance to mind your own thoughts and talk about yourself and your abilities.

16. Help others

When you help someone and do something good for someone else you feel more powerful, more important and your self-confidence grows. So helping others positively affects your self-confidence. It doesn't mean that you should sacrifice yourself for others, but in situations when you are able to help others, you should give them a hand. It won't cost you much, but it will mean a lot to somebody. Some of you might ask, "Why should I help others when they don't know how to appreciate it? If he were in my shoes, I'm sure he wouldn't help me". You are probably right thinking that some people might not be able to appreciate your help and do the same for you. However, helping people has a positive effect on your self-confidence and that is the most valuable thing you get at the moment.

17. Take care of your health

Health is not everything, but without health everything becomes nothing. Make sure you draw a plan of activities and nutrition which you will stick to in order to preserve your physical and mental health. Just as you must use your muscles to keep them in good shape, it's also important to "train" your brain, and this could include the following activities: reading, solving crossword puzzles, matching puzzles, playing chess... Good physical condition and a clear mind have a positive impact on self-confidence.

18. Take care of your physical appearance

A properly dressed person is usually described as self-confident, but this is often far from the truth. It is not rare that this facade hides a very insecure person, who tries to cover up the uncertainty by means of nice clothes. There are women who dare not leave their apartments, not even to take out the garbage, without having full makeup on their faces. It is clear that a good appearance is not enough to strengthen self-confidence. But here's why I still think it important to pay attention to physical appearance. Like it or not, other people make their first impressions of us and estimate us mostly based on our looks and appearance. A decently dressed person, with trimmed nails, neat hair, healthy and beautiful teeth always leaves a positive impression. Such individuals are more likely to attract the opposite sex, leave a better impression on employers, attract customers to make a purchase etc. than the ones who look plain and neglected no matter what other qualities they have. This is because the first impression that a person leaves is mostly based on their appearance. In addition, in certain situations, good clothes and a nice hairstyle can significantly help us feel self-confident. Here's what a twenty seven year old girl says: "Only when I wear this dress do I feel attractive and it is easy for me to flirt with guys. I can't imagine doing it in a sweat suit". Don't get me wrong, I do not suggest that you wear only costly, designer clothes, and always look tip-top with the newest hairstyle, looking like a Christmas tree. That is certainly not the point. The point is to customize your looks in accordance with the situation (workouts, business meetings, weddings...) and to wear what makes you feel self-confident. And it's all a matter of taste. Someone feels self-confident in one type of clothes, but someone else does not. Thus, some women say that wearing high heels makes a positive effect on their self-confidence, while others feel insecure because they do not even know how to walk in them properly. In short, try to look nice and well groomed, and wear what makes you feel good. Use the power of good appearance. Let it be the tool for your self-confidence strengthening.

19. Pay attention to your posture

In order to leave a good first impression on others when they see you, it is necessary to have the right posture. Lift your head, straighten your body, walk the steady pace, establish eye contact during communication with someone, speak loudly and clearly, offer a strong handshake. Regular physical training will ensure that your body is straight and strong. Eye contact is best practiced by watching your interlocutor at the base of his nose, just between their eyes. This way their eyes can't distract you, and they will have an impression that you are watching them straight in the eye. In order to speak loudly and clearly, practice reading books aloud – this will also help you to improve your communication skills.

5 WHAT WILL YOU ACCOMPLISH BY BUILDING YOUR SELF-CONFIDENCE?

After reading all these tips, I believe that some of you already have an idea of what specific steps to take to increase your self-confidence and have a few plans in mind. But we are not all the same. Some people are enterprising, easier to get themselves going and more motivated to action than others. On the contrary, some of you will think that everything seems fine in theory, written on paper, that it is too hard to make any progress and keep going as before. So let's do something about motivation. Let's see why it is good for you to increase your self-confidence. What to expect when you have finally managed to boost your self-confidence?

You will know yourself better

Self-image is the way people see themselves, how they perceive and describe themselves. Having your self-confidence increased, you will gain a positive self-image. You will become more aware of your own strengths and limitations, have better communication with yourself and much more faith in yourself.

You will be happier

People with high self-esteem like who they are. They feel good even being alone because their happiness does not depend on other people. As a self-confident person, you will love yourself, you will be self-satisfied and therefore you will be happier.

It will be easier for you to make decisions

The more self-confident you are, the more aware of your abilities, strengths and limitations you will be. You will always know what you can do, what you are good at, and what else you need to learn in order to be even better. This will contribute to your ability to recognize and to a greater extent use your potential and help you make important decisions.

You will gain an optimistic attitude towards life and achievement of your goals

By working on your self-confidence you replace the negative thoughts with positive ones ("I can do it"). You gain an optimistic attitude towards life and believe that problems can be solved. You expect good experiences and outcomes, and do not waste energy worrying about a possible negative outcome.

You will be ready to take risks

The greater your self-confidence, the more willing to take risks you will be. The more risks you are ready to take, the more chances for making progress you will have.

You will have potential to be a leader

When you are certain of yourself and your potential, and when it is easy for you to make decisions and take risks, you will be more adept in communication with others, and this will increase the chances of you becoming a leader.

You will become more responsible

You primarily rely on yourself and your abilities. You do not look for the causes of failure in other people or in extenuating circumstances.

You will be able to cope with stressful situations more easily

You will not be gloomy and bitter, but also not too idealistic and unrealistic. You will learn how to deal with problems. Having more self-confidence, you become surer of yourself and you will be less shaken by problematic life situations.

You will have a better chance of finding a partner and doing well in relationships

As a self-confident person you know yourself well, you know exactly what you want and what kind of partner suits you best. Since you are determined and willing to take risks, you have a greater chance of meeting the most suitable partner. Even more, your emotional stability and skills in intercourse with other people are all in favor of maintaining a good relationship.

You will be a successful parent

Being better to yourself, you will be also better to your child. As a self-confident person, you will set a good example to your child. Among other things, children also learn by copying a role model, by imitating their parents. As a self-confident parent, you are able to raise self-confident children.

You will be more creative

Being sure of yourself and your potential, you are able to be creative and use your imagination when solving problems.

6 INSTEAD OF A CONCLUSION

Now, compare the achievements of being self-confident with the problems caused by the lack of self-confidence described on the first pages of this manual. I believe that there is nothing more to be said to convince you to start building your self-confidence as soon as possible. Remember, you already made the first step by reading these lines. And yet, it is wrong to think: "Well, tomorrow or next Monday I am going to start applying what I've read in this guide." Believe me, there will be a much greater effect if you start applying it right now. And what is it that you can do right now? You can start by immediately taking a piece of paper and writing down your good qualities, everything you are proud of and what you have achieved in life so far. Keep this paper at a conspicuous spot to remind you how good and successful you are. Pick a visible spot to hang your diplomas, certificates, letters of thanks... anything that you have as proof of your successes. It is important to do something that will help you strengthen your self-confidence every single day even if it were just a small step that will not take up much of your time. How much you will be able to strengthen your self-confidence depends solely on you. Trust me, you can rely on yourself much more than you can imagine. The will and perseverance make miracles. The purpose of this manual is to give you the guidelines, to help you and contribute to your self-confidence building, but everything depends on you. The manual offers no magic recipes and quick fixes because they do not exist. If there were instant solutions, people wouldn't talk so much about this topic and show this much interest in problems caused by a lack of self-confidence, but they would solve them on their own in a short while. Self-confidence building is not an easy task. It needs a lot of time, effort, relinquishing the current way of life and habits, strong will and determination to persevere. But it is definitely possible. Just as you can influence your physical condition and stamina, improve your mental functions and appearance, you can also influence your self-confidence. The hardest thing is to begin. But once you grab the momentum and get yourself moving, it will be easier day after day. Having accomplished your first goal, you will get the wings and head on for the next one. Just give it a try, you have nothing to lose, but you can win a lot! By making an effort to build your self-confidence, you will feel much better than now and this feeling will be stronger day after day. Good luck!

ABOUT THE AUTHOR

Branka Vasilev was born in 1981 in Croatia, a small country in Europe. She is a psychologist with over six years experience, including four years as a member of the Team for children and youth protection at the Center for social affairs, and two years dealing with different profiles of workers in industrial environment. She also completed Basic course in Transactional Analysis – TA 101. She performed individual and group counseling including the following topics: external and internal self-confidence, assertive behavior, nonviolent conflict resolution, stress control etc. and was also helping people by giving advice as a free online counselor. Branka is happily married with one child.